Management
Tips 2

Harvard Business Review | Management Tips 2

Harvard Business Review Press

Boston, Massachusetts

Copyright 2021 Harvard Business School Publishing Corporation

All rights reserved
Printed in the United States of America
10 9 8 7 6 5 4 3 2 1

No part of this publication may be reproduced, stored in or introduced into a retrieval system, or transmitted, in any form, or by any means (electronic, mechanical, photocopying, recording, or otherwise), without the prior permission of the publisher. Requests for permission should be directed to permissions@harvardbusiness.org, or mailed to Permissions, Harvard Business School Publishing, 60 Harvard Way, Boston, Massachusetts 02163.

The web addresses referenced in this book were live and correct at the time of the book's publication but may be subject to change.

Library of Congress Cataloging-in-Publication Data

Names: Harvard Business Review Press, author.
Title: Management tips 2 / by Harvard Business Review.
Other titles: Management tips two
Description: Boston, Massachusetts : Harvard Business Review Press, [2020]
    |Includes index.
Identifiers: LCCN 2020026909 (print) | LCCN 2020026910 (ebook) |
    ISBN 9781647820145 (hardback) | ISBN 9781647820152 (ebook)
Subjects: LCSH: Management. | Leadership. | Success in business.
Classification: LCC HD31.2 H364 2020 (print) | LCC HD31.2 (ebook) | DDC
    658—dc23
LC record available at https://lccn.loc.gov/2020026909
LC ebook record available at https://lccn.loc.gov/2020026910

The paper used in this publication meets the requirements of the American National Standard for Permanence of Paper for Publications and Documents in Libraries and Archives Z39.48-1992.

Contents

About the Book

Management Tips 2 is a compilation of the Management Tip of the Day by *Harvard Business Review*. Adapted from digital articles and other content, these tips offer quick and practical advice on how to manage yourself and your team. Please turn to the list of attributions at the back of the book for more information on the sources from which these tips were adapted, and visit hbr.org for more tips and content.

Managing
Yourself

Know and Live by Your Personal Philosophy

Worrying about what other people think of us can be paralyzing. We stop taking chances and play it safe. Our careers suffer. To fight these anxieties, develop a personal philosophy that articulates your sense of who you are. What values drive your actions? Who has qualities that align with yours, and what are they? What makes you feel that you're performing at your best? How do you want to live your life? Write down your answers and look for what they have in common. Use the words that stand out to come up with your personal philosophy. Then commit to living by it. When something at work starts to lower your confidence, let your philosophy remind you of why you do what you do. Shut out others' opinions and focus on the things that really matter.

02

Lead Confidently When You Aren't Feeling Confident

When faced with a tough challenge, you may feel uncertain and even afraid. But it's hard to inspire your team if they sense that you're intimidated. You can project confidence by doing four things. First, demonstrate empathy for your team members. They want to know that you aren't out of touch with their feelings. Second, communicate your vision for the team and that tough challenge. People need to have a clear sense of where they are headed. Third, set a direction. Show the team how you'll reach the vision together. Last, give people proof so they have a reason to buy in to what you're telling them. Offer evidence for your direction and optimism. Be specific, be personal, and reference the work that the team is already doing to build their confidence and your own.

Improve Your Critical Thinking

To make good decisions, think critically. Too many leaders accept the first solution proposed or don't evaluate a topic from all sides. To guard against these mistakes, you can hone your critical thinking skills. First, question your assumptions, especially when the stakes are high. If you're coming up with a new business strategy, for example, ask: Why is this the best way forward? What does the research say about our expectations for the future of the market? Second, poke at the logic. When evaluating arguments, consider if the evidence builds up to a sound conclusion. Is the logic supported by data at each point? Third, seek fresh perspectives. Relying on your inner circle to help you think through these questions won't be productive if they all look and think like you. Ask other people to question and challenge your logic.

04

Focus on "Microhabits"

High achievers often have lofty aspirations for self-improvement. But big goals such as "meditate for an hour every day" or "read more" are often more burdensome than sustainable. So, start small by focusing on "microhabits," more achievable behaviors that you build over a long time. These habits should be ridiculously small, like meditating for thirty seconds or reading a paragraph each night. Piggyback on a daily task. Perform your new action at the same time as (or right before) something you already do every day. Read that one paragraph while brushing your teeth. Meditate while waiting for your coffee to brew. Then, track your progress, but keep it simple. Try using a "yes list" where you write down the desired action, and under each date, simply note a Y or N to indicate if you completed the task. Once you've accrued several weeks of Ys, you can increase your microhabit by a small increment, say 10 percent. Continue these incremental adjustments until the new habit is part of your muscle memory. By starting small, you can achieve big results.

05

Don't Let Perfectionism Get in Your Way

Perfectionism can push you to excellence, but it can also increase your anxiety and lower your productivity. Learn when to let go and move on. Create a checklist of a task's essentials. If you're working on a client pitch, for example, make sure the presentation addresses the client's major concerns and details why the client should hire your company. Your inner perfectionist might fret over the font choice and every semicolon, but once your checklist is complete, slowly back away. Or ask a trusted colleague to help you get perspective. Do you need someone to tell you when your first draft is good enough or when you should stop nitpicking? High standards are great, but they shouldn't keep you from getting your work done.

Don't Feel Guilty about Being Behind

When you have a never-ending to-do list, it's easy to feel guilty about what you haven't finished. But guilt is useful only when it motivates you to get more done—it shouldn't make you feel ashamed. To ease these kinds of emotions when they arise, exercise self-compassion. Imagine what you'd say to a friend who felt bad for being behind on a few projects. Chances are you'd tell your friend not to worry about it so much, so tell yourself the same thing. You can also make yourself feel better by focusing on what you *have* been able to accomplish. Keep a "done list" in addition to your to-do list, so you can remind yourself of past work. Remember that all that work you have to do will be there tomorrow, whether you feel guilty about it or not. So, cut yourself some slack, take a breath, and just do your best.

07

Clean Up Your Desk

If your workspace is a mess, you might be too. Research shows clutter adds to our stress and anxiety levels, detracts from our ability to focus, and makes us seem less conscientious and agreeable. Make a habit of tidying your workspace. Block off a few minutes on your calendar every week to sort through your piles of stuff. When it comes to managing digital clutter, ask IT for tools to organize online documents and advice on which items you can discard. For your home workspace, set up a designated area so that you have a boundary between work items and home items. (Research has also found that messy environments can encourage creativity; you just don't want your desk to get too chaotic.)

It's OK to Feel Uncomfortable When Learning

Being a beginner at something can feel awkward and embarrassing, especially if you're used to being an expert. But those feelings are inescapable growth pains that come from developing and improving. To get used to the discomfort, know that it's brave to be a beginner. Exposing your weaknesses and trying new things takes courage. Make the challenge a bit easier by looking for learning situations with low stakes—maybe a class where you're not expected to be an expert or you don't know anyone else. If it helps, tell fellow participants that you may mess up whatever you're about to attempt. Your willingness to take risks may inspire others to do the same. Don't stop learning. Keep pushing yourself, especially in the areas where you are accomplished, so you can get even better. If you are willing to feel embarrassment and shame, and even to fail, there's no end to what you can do.

09

Weave Learning into Your Everyday Work

We all need to keep learning new things to grow in our careers. But sometimes the urgency of our schedules gets in the way. To find time for learning, make it a part of your day-to-day tasks. Pick up skills from those around you. Notice how your boss handles a negotiation; ask salespeople about industry trends; get feedback from your peers after you give a presentation. At times, something may pique your interest, but you're too busy to explore it. Try creating a "to-learn" list: write down concepts, ideas, and practices that you want to return to later. And create a learning channel for your team, whether it's through Slack, SharePoint, or somewhere else, where you add links to valuable resources.

10

Move Past Your Mistakes

When you make a mistake at work, do you replay it in your head for days or even weeks? This overthinking is called rumination and can lead to serious anxiety. To break out of the cycle, identify your rumination triggers. Do certain types of people, projects, or decisions make you second-guess yourself? Notice when (and why) a situation is causing you to start overthinking. Distance yourself from negative thoughts by labeling them as *thoughts* or *feelings*. Instead of saying "I'm inadequate," say "I'm *feeling* like I'm inadequate." These labels help you distinguish what you're experiencing from who you are as a person and an employee. Distract yourself. When your brain won't stop spinning, do any simple activity you can focus on for a few minutes, like taking a walk or meditating.

11

Don't Take Small Annoyances at Work Personally

Sometimes the smallest action, or inaction, can have a big effect on how we feel about our colleagues. Imagine that you emailed a coworker days ago and they haven't replied. You might think the person is being rude, but they may just be under a tight deadline and feel bad about the delay. When you encounter situations, consider their broader context before jumping to conclusions. When a colleague's behavior is affecting you negatively, ask yourself if they could be focused on an important project for the boss. Is something in their personal life distracting them? How would the situation look to an outside observer? Is anything amiss or just seem that way because you're caught up in it? Assume the best about people—and try not to take things personally.

How to Handle Tough Feedback

When feedback is unexpectedly harsh, your first instinct may be to run and hide. Four steps can help you react productively:

1. *Collect yourself.* Breathe deeply and notice how you're feeling. Silently labeling your emotions ("I'm feeling hurt and ashamed") can help you distance yourself.

2. *Understand.* Ask the other person for detailed examples of the behavior high-lighted. Listen calmly, as if the conversation is about someone else.

3. *Recover.* Tell the person that you need to reflect and will respond when you can. Don't agree or disagree right away with what you've heard. Take some time to process and evaluate it.

4. *Engage.* Think about the validity of the feedback. Even tough criticism usually has a kernel of truth, so look for it. Then, share your thoughts with the person again.

13

Study Positive Feedback

Because critical feedback is jarring and threatening, it tends to stick in our brains. But positive feedback is invaluable for learning about your strengths and growth areas. Save the praise you get, anything from thank-you cards to written notes in your evaluations to comments in email threads. When you get mixed feedback, tease apart the positive and negative aspects, and put the positive ones in your kudos folder as well. Periodically review and reflect on what you've saved. What patterns or themes can you identify? How could you use your strengths in new situations? What else can you learn about your strengths, and who might provide that perspective? You may feel immodest or uncomfortable basking in positive feedback. But someone has gone out of their way to highlight what you're good at, so use it.

14

Create Space for Honesty

One way to get feedback that will help you improve is to build a culture where it's safe for employees to be honest. Show colleagues that you want to know what they think, especially when they might hesitate to tell you. Ask open-ended questions and listen carefully to the answers: "What did you hear when I shared my strategy?" or "How did it feel to you when I sent that email?" Tell your team that you want both positive and negative comments, and then resist the urge to respond to what they say; even if you disagree, simply listen and reflect. Thank your team for their honesty and use their feedback to make necessary changes.

Where Are You in Your Career? Where Do You Want to Go?

If you're not always clear how you should think about growing in your career, try writing a "from/to" statement that articulates where you are today and where you want to go. For example: "I want to progress *from* an individual contributor who adds value through technical expertise and closely follows others' directions, *to* a people leader who creates a clear strategy and delivers results through a small team." To write a from/to, ask trusted superiors and colleagues for their candid view of your current role and goals. Ask them to be brutally honest, because their transparency will help you figure out how you need to grow. Reflect on their answers and incorporate them into your from/to statement and then have your advisers read it to provide a reality check. Sometimes people think they're far ahead of where they are or choose an unrealistic destination.

16

Build Your Career While You Wait for Your Dream Job

When you're starting your career, should you hold out for your dream job or take anything you can get? The answer is "a little of each." There is value to be had from almost any role, so while you search for that ideal match, pay the bills with jobs that give you one (or more) of three things: experience, credibility, or income. You'll need the right skills and background to land your dream job, so in the meantime, look for roles that will let you build relevant experience. And consider jobs at companies with great reputations, even if the job in question isn't your exact goal. Having a top company on your résumé will make you stand out both now and in the future. Of course, sometimes you just need a paycheck. When all else fails, do what it takes to duct-tape an income together.

17

Get Mid-Career Help from a Mentor

Why do people get trapped in a mid-career rut? In some cases, after succeeding early on, they play it safe rather than taking the risks that would help them advance. As a result, they feel stuck in the status quo. If this situation sounds familiar, don't just hope things will change—get help. Find a trustworthy mentor who has navigated the same challenges. During your meetings together, discuss the tough work situations you're facing, and ask about their experiences and how they push themselves to keep growing. You could also find an executive coach to meet with regularly. A good coach will help you understand what's holding you back and explore options for your future. And do some reflecting on your own, too. Think about whether you still get satisfaction from your job, whether you're playing it safe, and where you want your career to go next.

18

Plan Your Retirement

If you want to continue working in some capacity after you retire, you'll have to plan. Ask yourself four questions:

- *How much money do I need to earn?* If a certain income is mandatory, this criterion has to come first and will influence your other decisions.

- *How much location independence do I want?* If you have visions of balancing some work with a lot of travel, or if you'd like to spend winters in sunny climes, think carefully about how to cultivate a location-independent second act, such as a seasonal or internet-enabled job.

- *How much change am I seeking?* If you'd simply like to downshift in your current career, ask your manager about transitioning into a consultant role. A bolder change will require additional groundwork.

- *How can I start test-driving my future career now?* Experiment with some small side projects while you have the security of your regular income.

19

Say No to Office Housework

No one likes to do "office housework"—low-importance tasks such as ordering lunch and taking notes in meetings. But research shows that certain groups of people, including women and people of color, are more likely to be assigned this kind of work, and that taking it on can hurt their careers. When faced with office housework, what should you do? First, have a prepared answer about how your time would be better spent: "I was hired to do X, and this new task would take away time from completing X well." For on-the-spot requests like ordering lunch, you might say, "I really need to be present during that meeting, as it's critical to what I'm working on." When you say no to housework, offer to do something of higher value instead. And if you can't say no, make sure that people are aware of the extra work you're doing and that you at least get credit for it.

20

Find Meaning in Tasks You Dislike

Think about an activity that you don't always enjoy doing—delivering performance reviews, for example. Now ask yourself why you do it but ask four times. The first time you ask "Why do I do this?" you might answer, "Because I have to" or "I want to let my people know where they stand." Then ask a second time: "Why do I want to let my people know where they stand?" The answer here might not be inspiring: "Because it's part of my job." But the answer might also start to sound more meaningful: "So that people can know how they can reach their career goals." Then ask a third time: "Why do I care if people know how to reach their career goals?" Continue for one more iteration. By the fourth round, you're likely to uncover a meaningful reason behind the activity—and a motivation for doing it well.

21

Schedule Breaks

The volume of information and stimuli coming at us every day makes it more difficult to focus than ever. To do the careful thinking that decision making and leadership require, you must step back from the noise of the world. Schedule fifteen-minute breaks at least once or twice a day to sit quietly in your office or take a walk. Commit to these breaks as you would any meeting or appointment; if you don't schedule moments of quiet, something else will fill the time. Use the time to think about your to-do list, especially the tasks you should stop doing. Solitude gives you the space to reflect on where your time is best spent. Try to get clarity on which meetings you should stop attending, which committees you should step down from, and which invitations you should politely decline.

22

Take Care of Your Body and Mind

Moving into a leadership position for the first time can be one of the most stressful moments in your career. To weather the transition, start by shifting your mindset. Focus on what excites you about the switch, not on what scares you. This will help you relax into your role and mitigate self-doubt. Practicing mindfulness techniques, such as meditation and controlled breathing, will develop your ability to stay calm and poised in challenging situations, such as running a contentious meeting or making a high-stakes decision. Lastly, you won't succeed unless you take time to care for your overall health. You may be strapped for time, but don't put off going to your annual medical checkup or finding a therapist if you've been struggling mentally. Sound sleep, regular exercise, good nutrition, and mental health are especially important when taking on a new role.

23

Stop Constantly Checking Your Phone

Focusing can be hard with all that beeping from your phone. There are simple ways to reduce distractions. Turn off push notifications. If that doesn't help, use airplane mode to limit interruptions when you're trying to focus. If being out of touch gives you anxiety, make exceptions for specific numbers, such as those of loved ones or important business colleagues. Check email, instant messages, social media, and text messages in batches, rather than sporadically throughout the day. Quickly checking anything, even for one-tenth of a second, can add up to major productivity losses; it can take an average of twenty-three minutes to get back in the zone after switching tasks. It's OK to not respond immediately. In addition to giving you more uninterrupted focus time, delaying can lead to better decision making by giving you more time to think about your response.

24

Practice Your Negotiation Skills

Whether you're seeking more money, higher status, increased visibility, additional resources, or more time off, you likely won't get it if you don't ask your boss for it. Make your request a win-win by using phrases that imply joint success, such as "How can we both do well?" Then respond with "what ifs." For example, if your boss says that you need more experience before you can advance, you might reply with an exact strategy: "What if I take the lead on our communications strategy with the sales team?" Even if you get an initial no, you can still leave the negotiation with a small win that may put you on the path to an eventual yes.

Break Out of a Creative Rut

Creativity can fade when you get bored or discouraged at work. To get your creative juices flowing again, change your habits. Try something new every month. Meet new people at work. Talk to new clients. Look for intersections—places where your department's work overlaps with another. Volunteer for a cross-functional activity. And seek obstacles as opportunities for research and analysis. (Why is it there? Whom does it serve? What are its effects? What are other ways of getting the results you're looking for?) Start by selecting obstacles you can change and continue on from there. Find ways to share what you know with others—write an article, lead a training session, or mentor a young upstart.

26

Make a Tough Decision Easier to Accept

When you're faced with a tough call, consider two things that make these decisions so difficult: *uncertainty* about the outcome and *value complexity*, the notion that any choice you make will negatively affect someone. To reduce the uncertainty in a decision, first consider the costs of not acting, and then think carefully about your options. Have you made any assumptions that are holding you back? Are there low-risk, small-scale ways to test your options? To handle value complexity, consider how you can help people understand your decision once you make it. Especially when the decision involves trade-offs that will affect others, you'll want to be as clear as possible about your intentions.

Block Off Your Schedule

You can't do deep, creative work when meetings constantly disrupt your flow and hurt your productivity. To have time and space to focus, establish one day a week when nothing can interrupt you—no texts, no emails, no phone calls, and absolutely no meetings. Block this day off on your calendar and tell colleagues that you'll be unreachable because you're working on critical projects. Something urgent may come up anyway but try to keep the day from being compromised. Stick to a simple rule: you can move your unreachable day around—maybe it's Wednesday one week and Thursday the next—but you can't remove it from your calendar or push it to the following week. As you get into the routine of taking days for focused work, it'll be easier for you, and the people around you, to keep them sacred.

28

Feel in Control to Avoid Burnout

There are many reasons people feel burned out at work—an overstuffed to-do list, tasks that seem meaningless, a lack of connection with others. One of the largest contributors to burnout is feeling that you lack control. If you don't have autonomy in your job or a say in the decisions that affect your professional life, it can take a toll on your well-being. When you find yourself feeling not in control, step back and ask why. Does your boss contact you at all hours, so you're always on call? Are the team's priorities constantly shifting, so you can never get ahead? Once you know the reasons, figure out what you can do to address them. Maybe you could establish better boundaries with your boss or get the team to agree that certain priorities will remain constant. Having control in even a few areas can help you avoid burnout later on.

Create Project Deadlines

How do you motivate yourself when a project doesn't have a deadline? Try making one up. Pick a date that you want the work done by or set aside some time for it each day or week. Create accountability by enlisting positive peer pressure. Tell a colleague what your deadline is (even if you picked it) and send them updates regularly. For additional motivation, incentivize yourself. For example, after spending a morning on the project, you might treat yourself to lunch. Or work from your favorite coffee shop, as long as you finish the project's next step. If those incentives aren't powerful enough, try penalties. Decide that if you don't complete the task as planned, you won't be able to listen to your favorite podcast or watch your favorite TV show tonight.

30

Don't Let Your To-Do List Distract You from Leading

If you're struggling to balance your individual work and the work of leading your team, reset your priorities. Seek out leaders who find that balance and ask how they do it. You can also ask them for feedback on your efforts. Use the feedback to think about ways you can give employees what they need, whether it's holding regular career development conversations, pausing to acknowledge a colleague's efforts, or closing your laptop to focus in one-on-one meetings. Over the next few weeks, notice when you feel a task or deadline pulling your attention away from a direct report. Remind yourself to focus on the people you're leading. You'll be able to get back to your to-do list soon enough.

Be More Efficient

Small changes to your work style could end up saving you hours each week. For instance, before eagerly jumping into a new project, talk to stakeholders about their expectations so that you know what to prioritize. Maybe they want a detailed project plan, but maybe a rough outline would get the job done, too. It's also helpful to ask yourself if you could reuse any past work to complete the project at hand. Say you're preparing a presentation to senior leaders. Can you pull language from the proposal it's based on or draw on other materials to flesh it out? Last, use "timeboxing" to organize your efforts. Decide in advance how long you will spend on each task and stick to it. Even if you don't finish everything in the allotted time, timeboxing will help you focus for short bursts of productivity.

32

Use Habits to Stay Grounded

When your life is disrupted by a big life event—a job change, a baby, a relative's illness—how do you maintain your focus and well-being? Add some stability to an unstable time by making sure your habits align with your long-term goals. Think about the five to ten things you need to do every week to keep your life on track and list them. Many critical habits fall into one of four areas: personal reflection, professional reflection, relationships, and health (both physical and mental). You should also think about how you'll create accountability for yourself. Will you post the list where you'll see it often? Use an app to set reminders? Check in with a friend each week? Creating and reinforcing habits this way can assure you that you're doing what you need to—no matter how many things you're juggling.

Set Goals That You Actually Want to Accomplish

You're unlikely to make progress on your professional development goals if they feel like a chore. Instead of focusing on things you "should" do, choose one or two areas of focus that align with what really matters to you. Ask yourself:

- If I could accomplish just one major professional development goal this year, what would it be?
- When I think about this goal, do I get excited about the prospect of working on it as well as achieving it?
- Do I want to achieve this goal because it's interesting and important or because I think it would please other people?

Use the answers to come up with a short list of goals that truly match your personal ambitions.

34

Stay Focused

Constant access to data is killing our productivity. We begin the day by picking up our phones and getting lost in a stream of notifications and information. You can do three things to carve out more time and remain focused and effective at work:

- *Start your day right.* When you wake up, don't start checking email on your phone. Try a simple mindfulness practice: take a few deep breaths, make a mental list of the things you're grateful for, or meditate for twenty to thirty minutes.
- *Organize your day.* Use your body's natural rhythms. Focus on complex, creative tasks in the morning. Push meetings to the afternoon.
- *Tidy up.* A clean work environment leads to a less cluttered mind. Put everything in a drawer. Create folders on your computer

desktop to get rid of all the random files. On your phone, keep only the eight to twelve most important apps on your home screen. Turn off all unnecessary notifications.

35

Try This If You're Constantly Overwhelmed

It's no surprise that many of us feel overwhelmed a lot of the time. If your to-do list never seems to get shorter, step back and try a new approach. Consider whether certain tasks are stressing you out more than others. If so, focus on those first: finish a big project as soon as possible or break down a complicated goal into more manageable steps. You should also consider whether perfectionist tendencies are getting in your way. Think about what "good enough" looks like, and be honest about whether spending more time on something will meaningfully improve it. (If not, take a breath and move on.) Finally, ask yourself which to-dos are truly a good use of your time—and then delegate those that aren't. Thinking about how you're using your time can help you use it more wisely.

Protect Your Nonwork Time

Some jobs have very clear lines between when you're "on" and when you're "off." But when you work in a role where the lines are blurred—or potentially nonexistent—it's important to protect your nonwork time. If you feel like work is taking over most of your waking hours, start by clearly defining what "after hours" means for you. Take into account the number of hours you're expected to work each week, as well as personal commitments like attending an exercise class you really enjoy. When do you need to start and stop to put in the appropriate amount of work time? Then, develop mental clarity about what needs to get done and when you will do it. Keep track of your tasks and plan them out. Make sure you block off time for an end-of-workday wrap-up, where you review and make sure you did everything you needed to do for the day. Last, communicate with your colleagues about how (or if) you want to be contacted during your off hours. Really guard your time. If you don't, you won't get the mental break that everyone needs.

Treat the Weekend Like a Vacation

When Monday morning arrives, do you feel relaxed? Or are you still stressed out from the previous week? Research shows that one way to make your weekends more refreshing is to think of them as a short vacation. Simply enjoy yourself: sleep in, do less housework, eat a bit more than you normally would. And find ways to make common tasks more fun, whether turning on upbeat music in the car while running errands or making yourself a margarita for folding laundry. Slow down: pay attention to your surroundings, your activity, and the people involved. Keeping your mind on whatever's happening will help you savor it, which in turn will help you feel as if you're breaking out of the day-to-day grind. But save these vacation weekends for when you really need them—research shows they lose their effects if they happen too often.

38

Make Time for Your Hobbies

When we don't make time for our hobbies, our professional lives pay a price. Why? First, hobbies awaken our creativity. It's hard to come up with new ideas at work when our brains are filled with targets and deadlines. A creative hobby pulls you out of that by giving you a blank canvas and mental space to make connections. Second, hobbies provide a fresh perspective. Part of coming up with ideas is imagining how people (say, customers) will react to them. If you write, paint, or make music, you're probably used to thinking about how a reader or listener will experience your work. Bring that mentality to your job, too. Last, hobbies bolster confidence. When a tough project has you feeling discouraged, taking an hour for a hobby can boost your confidence and mood. Use that boost to tackle the project with fresh resolve.

39

Be an Attentive Mentor

How can you make sure your schedule full of meetings and obligations doesn't hinder your ability to be an attentive mentor? First, appreciate that some time is better than none. If sixty-minute meetings aren't possible, try to set aside thirty or even fifteen minutes. These smaller windows will force your mentee (and you) to get to the point. Be fully present and engaged during mentoring sessions. Whether you are meeting in person, over Skype, or by text, demonstrate to your mentee that for the next few minutes, they are all that matters. If you get distracted by other tasks or your next meeting, refocus and remind yourself to be here, now.

40

Improve Your Emotional Intelligence

It's not always obvious how to improve your emotional intelligence skills, especially because we often don't know how others perceive us. To figure out where you can improve, start with a reality check: What are the major differences between how you see yourself and how others see you? You can get this kind of feedback from a 360-degree assessment, a coach, or a skilled manager. Next, consider your goals. Do you want to eventually take on a leadership position? Be a better team member? Consider how your ambitions match up with the skills that others think you need to improve. Then identify specific actions that you'll take to improve those skills. Working on becoming a better listener? You might decide that when you're talking with someone, you won't reply until you've taken the time to pause and check that you understand what they said. Whatever skill you decide to improve, use every opportunity to practice it, no matter how small.

41

Don't Overuse Your Strengths

Most leaders have strengths that make them distinctive. But those same characteristics, when overused, can have a downside. For example, a well-honed sense of self-control can turn into rigidity. Courage, taken to the extreme, might become recklessness. Honesty, if not tempered, can turn into cruelty. Take some time to think about which of your skills you might be relying on too much. For example, consider one of your strengths that has served you well at work and that others have admired. Then try to recall a situation in which you relied on that quality more than you should have. Are there occasions when your strength became a liability, causing more harm than good and perhaps even leading to an unintended outcome? Keep in mind that we tend to overuse our strengths under stress. When we're not getting what we want, our instinct is to double down on whatever has worked best in the past.

42

Know Which Skills Can Take You to a New Career

One of the hardest parts of switching careers is knowing which of your skills you can apply in a new way. Many industries may value your talents as much as your current one does. Here's how to identify your transplantable core skills:

- *Tap other reinventors.* Consult with people who have already transitioned from your industry to a different career. Discuss what core skills you might be overlooking and how they could apply elsewhere.

- *Confer with outsiders.* Talk with a wide range of folks outside your industry. Ask them about your core skills. How you should market them? What less-obvious functions or organizations are looking for such skills? What are the obstacles to landing such work?

- *Create a strategic message.* Distill your goals and skills into a simple statement to guide you. For example: "Communicate clearly, execute fast, think creatively, and act with courage."

43

Build Your Personal Brand

Developing a reputation as an expert can lead to promotions and new assignments and also open up other professional opportunities. You don't have to be a worldwide expert right away. You can coach others on writing better business memos even if you aren't Shakespeare. Be clear about what you do—and don't—know. Being honest that you have some knowledge and are acquiring more will lead others to respect you. And make sure your company understands the value of your public brand. Particularly if your expertise isn't part of your core responsibilities, show your manager how your more visible profile can help the company. Strategically expand what you're known for. Emphasize your full range of talents so that your new expertise doesn't pigeonhole you.

Stop Underpricing Your Freelance Work

Overpricing your work can scare clients away. But charging low prices can signal low quality, making clients hesitate to work with you. To ensure you aren't underselling yourself, ask trusted peers to provide honest information about going rates. Once you know what your price should be, practice saying it out loud. Quoting a fee to a client can be nerve-racking, especially a rate increase but rehearsing it will make you more confident. Then test the market demand for your new rate and adjust accordingly. Increase your price steadily and incrementally until you feel you're earning what you deserve. If you ask for a rate that clients resist, consider freezing or reducing your rate until you've built up other income streams or increased your reputation. Asking for what you deserve gets you not only more money but also more respect.

45

On Social Media, Be Polite and Get to the Point

Social media is an effective tool for expanding your network but reaching out to people you don't know can be awkward. You'll have a better chance of success if you prioritize people who are close to your level in their careers. This network will grow in seniority with you and can connect you with opportunities down the line—and peers are more likely to respond than someone in the C-suite anyway. Make sure your initial message is brief and personal; approach it as you would a handwritten note. Think of the three points you want to convey, and let your natural voice come through. If you and the person have something in common, like a shared interest or mutual friend, mention it. It's also a good idea to be direct (and polite) about what you're looking for. If you're seeking advice, for example, you can say, "I'm struggling with a business problem and would love to find out what you think."

46

Don't Let a Long Job Search Get You Down

Start by acknowledging that there will be ups and downs. Remind yourself that long waits, and the emotions they cause, are normal. Activities like mindful meditation and journaling can help you experience and sort through your feelings in a positive way. You may also want to enlist the help of a coach, therapist, or work group for support. If you're unemployed, be sure to do activities that energize you, such as exercising or having lunch with a friend. And don't take delays personally. If a contact hasn't made the introduction that they promised, send a friendly reminder, but also think about their other priorities. Chances are, the person wants to help you—they're just busy.

If You Mess Up a Job Interview, Fix Your Mistake

Job interviews are stressful. Even when you've done a ton of preparation and practiced your answers, the pressure might cause you to say the wrong thing, respond to a question incompletely, or leave out a critical piece of information. You can't ask for a do-over, but you can try to correct your mistake. If you're still in the interview, you might politely say: "I just realized that I haven't mentioned . . . " or "I don't think I fully answered your question. I'd like to add . . . " If you realize your mistake or omission after the interview, you can send a thank-you email that says, "I want to add to [or clarify, or revise] what I said about X . . . " Then you don't have to worry about your flub. You can know that you did your best—and that it's now up to the hiring manager.

48

Stay Focused in a New Job

Your first few months in a job have a major impact on whether you succeed. Many people have trouble deciding where to focus their energy early on, so use three questions to guide you.

- *How will I create value?* Know what is expected of you, by when, and how your progress is assessed. Consider the interests of all stakeholders (not just your boss), and keep in mind that the answer may shift over time.

- *Whose support is critical?* The company has a political landscape—learn to navigate it. Learn who has power and influence, and then build alliances with them. If you can help them accomplish their goals, they may return the favor.

- *What skills do I need?* The abilities that got you the job may not be the same ones you need now. The sooner you understand what you should acquire and develop, the better.

49

Show How a New Job Title Will Benefit the Company

If you've been in your job for a few years, you've probably seen your responsibilities expand. But if your job title hasn't changed, talk to your boss. Before you ask for a title change, ask yourself, "What would help my manager say yes?" Think carefully about why you deserve a new title— maybe you just sealed a big new deal for the company, or you executed an important project—and how it will help you be more effective in your job. Will it give you more credibility with your colleagues? Help you build rapport with clients? Grant you more authority to make decisions? Consider what your supervisor cares and worries about most and use that to build your case. Your boss is more likely to agree when the change benefits you *and* the company.

Take Charge of Your New Role after a Promotion

Moving up in an organization usually means greater rewards, more responsibilities, and higher stakes. But transitioning into a bigger role can be challenging. Typically, the more senior the role, the less structured the onboarding process, which can feel disorienting. The key is to take responsibility for it yourself. You can ask for help or accept support, but you should get up to speed as independently as possible. Start by answering these questions:

- What do I need to do in the first week? The first thirty days? The first quarter?
- Who do I need to meet, and what's the best way to connect with them?

- What don't I know—and what will I be expected to know?
- If I find myself struggling, how will I ask for help or guidance?

Be Your Own Advocate

A good boss can guide your career, but they can also leave you floundering if they won't support you. If you're struggling to get the help you need to move up, take your career into your own hands. Developing a group of mentors is a good way to start. Put together a team of people to support you, both inside and outside your organization. Think broadly across levels and functions. Look for people whose careers are further along than yours and whose style or achievements you admire. You should also find ways to make yourself visible to important stakeholders in the company—your boss's boss, for example. Volunteer to work on cross-functional projects that senior leaders will have their eye on. And keep in mind that building your status outside the organization often gains you visibility inside it. You might decide to join an industry association and work toward a leadership position there, for example, or use social media to engage with top thinkers in your field.

Ask for a Raise at the Right Time

Most people make their pitch for a raise at review time, when their bosses are often overwhelmed with the pressure of completing evaluations. Instead, time your request to coincide with changes in your own tasks. You should ask for a raise just before you take on new responsibilities or right after you successfully complete a project. If you've just created more value for your company, it's a great time to say, "Can we share that value?" If you've collected evidence about your contributions and have a reasonable target figure in mind, you're more likely to get what you want. Just make sure to look forward, not backward. You want to highlight your contributions, but then you should pivot to what you hope to tackle next. If your boss doesn't seem receptive, suggest revisiting the issue in a few months and then get that on their calendar.

53

Prepare for Tough Conversations

Difficult conversations are never fun, but preparing for them can help you ensure they're productive. Start by identifying your motives. What do you want out of the conversation—for you, the other person, and any stakeholders involved? Knowing your goals is a good way to keep the meeting on track if emotions rise. Next, gather facts to support your position. If you're about to ask for a raise, for example, write down notes on how you've grown in your role. If you're going to give someone tough feedback, bring examples of their work and behavior. Be ready to defend your point of view and explain how you came to it. And think through any stories you're telling yourself about the other person. Do you see your boss as "the enemy" because she can grant or deny your raise request? Consider what your manager will care about in the conversation and use that to plan how you'll address their concerns.

54

Stay Calm during a Tough Conversation

Having a tense conversation brings up a lot of negative emotions, leaving you feeling like an active volcano. To prevent an outburst and stay in control of your emotions, physically ground yourself in your environment. One of the best ways to do this is to stand up and walk around, which activates the thinking part of your brain. If you and your counterpart are seated at a table, and suddenly standing up seems awkward, you might say, "I feel like I need to stretch. Mind if I walk around a bit?" If that doesn't feel comfortable, you can do small physical things like crossing two fingers or placing your feet firmly on the floor and noticing what it feels like. Mindfulness experts call these actions "anchoring." Whatever you can do to focus on your physical presence and your senses will help you stay grounded and get through that tough conversation.

Rehearse Your Presentations

Before a critical presentation, the best thing you can do is rehearse—a lot. You don't need to memorize every line (which will make you sound *too* rehearsed). Your goal should be to speak confidently while leaving room for spontaneity. Spend extra time on the beginning and end of your talk, including your first and last slides. The introduction sets the stage for your message and gives your audience a reason to care. Your conclusion determines which ideas people will walk away with. If you nail these two sections of the talk, you'll probably do well. You should also repeatedly practice any sections that have complex or technical content. While you rehearse, record yourself on your phone; play it back to watch for distracting habits (fidgeting, avoiding eye contact) and areas where you seem unsure. Rehearse those sections a few more times.

56

Give a Persuasive Presentation

When you need to sell an idea at work or in a presentation, how do you do it? Five rhetorical devices can help. Aristotle identified them two thousand years ago, and masters of persuasion still use them:

- *Ethos.* Start your talk by establishing your credibility and character. Show your audience that you are committed to the welfare of others, and you will gain their trust.
- *Logos.* Use data, evidence, and facts to support your pitch.
- *Pathos.* People are moved to action by how a speaker makes them feel. Wrap your big idea in a story that will elicit an emotional reaction.
- *Metaphor.* Comparing your idea to something familiar to your audience clarifies

your argument by making the abstract
concrete.

- *Brevity.* Explain your idea in as few words
  as possible. People have a limited attention
  span, so talk about your strongest points
  first.

Connect with Your Audience Remotely

Good presenters know how to connect with their audience, which is really challenging in a virtual setting. To start, you have to adopt an engaged, active persona. Make eye contact with your participants by looking directly into the camera as often as possible. This can be hard to remember, especially if you have to look elsewhere on your screen to see the participants. To make it easier, set up your screen so that the window with your audience is close to the camera. This way you can simultaneously make eye contact with them and see their response. Pay attention to the angle of the camera so your face is at a comfortable level for others to see you. Remember to show a warm, engaging smile; laugh occasionally; and maintain a friendly, engaging tone. In informal meetings, you might create a connection by turning the camera on your dog laying by your feet. In more formal settings, you can start the meeting with a personal story or ask people to talk about where they're calling from to create a sense of warmth and connection.

58

Run a Good Meeting by Getting the Basics Right

Plenty of meetings are a waste of time. They're unfocused, badly run, and way too long. But improving your meetings isn't rocket science—work on getting the basics right. When planning a meeting, know why you are scheduling it in the first place. Having a specific goal in mind will help you create a useful agenda. Next, decide who truly needs to be there, considering the key decision makers, influencers, and stakeholders. If certain people should be in the loop but don't need to attend, you can ask for their input beforehand and update them afterward. Open the meeting by clearly laying out its purpose and focusing people on the task at hand. As the facilitator, your role is to get attendees to feel committed to the outcome.

When the meeting is over, take a few minutes to reflect. Did everyone participate? Were people distracted? What worked well, and what didn't? Use your reflections (ask others for their thoughts, too) to keep improving for next time.

59

Speak Up in Meetings

Speaking up in a meeting can increase your visibility at work, but isn't natural for everyone. If you struggle to offer your thoughts on the spot, you can prepare a few comments or questions so that you know you'll have something to say. Also think about your reasons for wanting to speak up in the first place. Ask yourself why you care about the meeting's topic and use the answer as inspiration when crafting your comments and questions. During the meeting, when your turn comes, pause and breathe. This can strengthen your voice, helping you to speak with clarity and authority. But, saying something just to talk isn't always a great idea. If you're speaking up to show off or to offer a comment that would be better expressed one-on-one with someone, it may be better to say nothing.

60

Surround Yourself with People Who Push You to Grow

When planning our careers, we carefully choose our companies and jobs. But rarely are we deliberate about selecting advisers and confidantes to help us succeed. Cultivate a support group for your career by considering who inspires you, whether colleagues, senior leaders, or peers in your field. Seek out these individuals and be candid about why you admire them and want to connect. Focus on building a relationship that will benefit both of you. As you get to know each other, don't be afraid to explore big life questions: What do you want to do with your life? What motivates you? What are you doing that you really don't like to do? Work together to become better versions of yourselves.

Managing
Your Team

Adapt Your Leadership Style to the Situation

Different work situations call for different leadership styles, and most managers use one of two approaches: dominance or prestige. When you lead through dominance, you influence others by being assertive and leveraging your power and formal authority. This approach works best when your job is to get everyone aligned and moving in the same direction. When there is a clear strategy for a new product launch, for example, and the challenge is in getting your team to enact that vision, dominance is an effective way to create a unified front. Prestige, in contrast, means influencing others by displaying signs of wisdom and expertise and being a role model. This approach works best when you're trying to empower the people who report to you. If a marketing team is charged with creating an innovative advertising campaign, for example, a prestigious leader can release the constraints on team members and encourage them to think outside the box.

02

Build Your Emotional Courage

Start by thinking of a leadership skill you want to get better at: giving feedback, listening, being direct—whatever you want to grow in. Then practice that skill in a low-risk situation. For example, let's say you want to get better at being direct. The next time there's a mistake on your phone bill, call customer service and practice being succinct and clear. Notice how you *want* to react— Get angry? Backpedal?—and focus on resisting those impulses. These are the same feelings you'll encounter in higher-risk situations at work, so learn to push through them. Continue to practice until you feel comfortable and can respond the way you'd like to.

03

You Don't Have to Be Isolated

If you're a senior executive, there's a good chance you're out of touch. Having a layer of handlers who decide what you should or shouldn't see may save you time, but it also keeps you isolated and disconnected. This is a serious problem. If you don't have firsthand information about your employees and customers, you're unlikely to make the best decisions. So get out of your bubble. Do a stint on the front line—answering customer service calls or handling a key client—so you get direct exposure to lower-level employees and the people who buy your products. Consider instituting skip-level meetings, where you can talk with lower-level teams (without their bosses present) about business conditions and customer reactions, and how to implement strategies. In all settings, encourage people to challenge your thinking instead of just saying what you want to hear.

04

Don't Let Your Ideas Overpower Your Team's

Your job as a leader is to create a safe space where your team can share ideas without fear of judgment. But knowing how to give input without squashing others' suggestions can be tough. Should you jump in with your own ideas during brainstorming sessions, or step back and be a coach? The key is to find the right balance. Deadlines and performance targets can increase the pressure to impose your own opinions, but doing so will increase your team's self-doubt and perpetuate the perception of the all-knowing leader. So take off your leader hat and convincingly tell your team not to treat your ideas any differently than their own. If you notice that your contributions mute their participation, return to coaching. Your team won't be creative if they are waiting for you to tell them what to do.

05

Prime Your Team for Creative Thinking

Innovative thinking is fueled when a wide range of talents, skills, and traits come together. If you want to enhance the creative potential of your team, develop the diversity of their skills. Here are a few ways to get started:

- *Build expertise.* Send your team to professional conferences, or arrange training sessions to help them gain new skills.
- *Take field trips.* Arrange a site visit to a customer or even to a competitor. Or observe best practices in an unfamiliar industry. For example, an airline hoping to improve customer service might visit a clothing retailer known for its excellence in that area.
- *Host creative events.* Bring in outside speakers to give talks or workshops.

- ***Seek additional resources.*** Gather your team to watch and discuss a TED talk, or form an ad hoc reading club to discuss books and articles of interest.

06

How to Manage Your Most Creative Employees

Some bosses wonder how to manage creative people. Research suggests that they may in fact have a different type of personality. But that doesn't mean you need to manage them in a completely different way; a lot of the same rules apply. Focus on making sure there's a good fit between their creative tendencies and their role, so you can tap into the full range of their talents. Surround them with detail-oriented project managers who will handle the implementation of their ideas. Don't worry if their approach to work is nothing like yours, as long as they're meeting deadlines. Prove that your company truly values creativity by rewarding people who come up with innovations. And apply the right amount of pressure to projects; too little will lead to a lack of motivation, and too much will create stress that inhibits creativity. Organizations that provide their most talented people with personalized development plans and mentoring opportunities, and that promote a culture of support and inclusion, will benefit from increased creative performance.

Don't Hide Your Weaknesses

You might be tempted to want colleagues to see you only at your best, but that's a bad way to lead. For one thing, it's unsustainable. We're all human, and we all make mistakes. Sooner or later, you will, too. For another, leading is about connecting. People will follow you, work hard for you, and sacrifice for you if they feel connected to you. And they won't feel that way if you only let them see what you think will impress them. So don't be afraid to own up to the areas where you aren't perfect. If it helps, think of it this way: you aren't weak; you have weaknesses. There is a difference.

Follow These Rules from the Best Bosses

Amazing bosses try to make work meaningful and enjoyable for employees. They're most successful when they adhere to a few best practices:

- *Manage individuals, not just teams.* When you're under pressure, you can forget that employees have varying interests, abilities, goals, and styles of learning. But it's important to understand what makes each person tick so that you can customize your interactions with them.
- *Go big on meaning.* Inspire people with a vision, set challenging goals, and articulate a clear purpose. Don't rely on incentives like bonuses, stock options, or raises.
- *Focus on feedback.* Use regular (at least weekly) one-on-one conversations for coaching. Make the feedback clear, honest, and constructive.

- *Don't just talk—listen.* Pose problems and challenges, and then ask questions to enlist the entire team in generating solutions.
- *Be consistent.* Be open to new ideas in your management style, vision, expectations, and feedback. If change becomes necessary, acknowledge it quickly.

09

Get More Out of One-on-One Meetings

One-on-one meetings often feel hurried and disorganized. To improve them, be deliberate about how you structure them. First, schedule them, so they are repeating events on your calendar. And honor these time slots. Don't cancel, which signals to your employee that you don't value their time. Make sure there's an agenda. Before the meeting, ask your direct report for a synopsis of what they'd like to talk about. You should do the same for them. During the meeting, be present. Turn off your phone; mute notifications. Start by complimenting your colleague on something they do well. Then, listen to your colleague's concerns and provide feedback and ideas on how they might solve problems. Always close with a note of appreciation.

10

Micromanagement Limits a Team's Growth

You may want to be kept in the loop, but micromanaging hurts morale, establishes mistrust, and limits your team's growth. Here's how to break the habit:

- *Understand why you do it.* Micromanaging often comes from insecurity. Think about the reasons you shouldn't micromanage.
- *Prioritize what actually matters.* Determine which tasks you truly need to do. The real work of leaders is to think strategically, not do their team's jobs for them.
- *Talk to your team.* Be clear about when you want updates on their work, so they can ease your anxiety. Ask them how you can better support them.

- ***Step back slowly.*** Tell your employees you trust them to make decisions. Try not to overreact when things don't go exactly as you'd like.

11

Admit Failure

As a leader, admitting failure is critical. Many people try to shrug off missteps as things that happen to everyone. Although doing so might seem harmless, there are many good reasons why you should admit you've messed up. Here are three:

- *To connect with your employees.* While most employees won't want to discuss their own failures, they are more likely to connect with leaders who admit to theirs. Even if the specific failure isn't applicable to staff, simply talking about it helps you connect.

- *To learn.* Failure is only positive when you learn something important from it and make the necessary adjustments. If you don't do this, you cannot learn from outside perspectives and you're more likely to stay in denial.

- *To tolerate mistakes in others.* As much as leaders openly say that failure must happen for innovation to be present, many get upset at staff who fail or struggle. That attitude shuts up staff, closes down experimentation, and obliterates creativity. Set an example that failure is OK.

Encourage Healthy Habits

Your job is to support your team through intense work periods. The first step is to take care of yourself: eat nutritious food, exercise, get plenty of sleep, and find a friend to vent to when you need it. These things aren't luxuries—a healthy mind and body will help you lead well. When you turn your attention to your team, think about how you can be compassionate, be a source of optimism, and set a good example. Show your employees that, whatever the stressful situation, you're all in it together. Talk about how you cope with stress, and encourage people to take breaks, improve their work-life balance, and maintain a healthy attitude toward daily work and deadlines. Remind people why their work is important to the company and to customers. Renewing your sense of purpose is a good way to fight the drain of burnout.

13

Use Celebrations to Mark Important Moments

People have long used ceremonies—bar mitzvahs, baptisms, weddings, quinceañeras—to mark changes and turning points. Companies have ceremonies too, but they often focus on celebrating the positive: work anniversaries, promotions, and project victories. These types of recognition are important and shouldn't stop, but companies should consider using celebrations to help people through hard times. This can be a powerful way to mark difficulties, acknowledge and honor those who have sacrificed or experienced hardship, and help people move on. You may not celebrate after a difficult reorg, but you might gather as a group and read your mission statement aloud. Communal experiences can help strengthen your group's bonds, values, and vision.

Help Your Employees Feel Purpose

Instilling purpose in your employees takes more than motivational talks, lofty speeches, or mission statements. In fact, if overblown or insincere, those methods can backfire, triggering cynicism rather than commitment. To inspire and engage your employees, keep two things in mind. First, purpose is a feeling. You could tell your team that their work is important, but how can you help individuals feel it firsthand? Think about ways to show people the impact of their jobs. Perhaps you could bring a customer in to share a testimonial, or send a small team into the field to experience the client's needs for themselves. Second, authenticity matters—a lot. If your attempts at creating purpose do not align with how you've acted in the past, employees will likely be skeptical, and they might be left feeling more manipulated than inspired. Making the pursuit of purpose a routine, rather than a one-off initiative, will show employees that you're serious about it.

Coach an Employee to Solve Problems in New Ways

Start off by asking a few questions: What problem are you solving? What concerns you about it? What frustrates other people about it? Your goal is to get the person thinking about why their efforts aren't working. Repeat their answers back to them. Once they understand why their plan of action is flawed, ask what else they might try, based on what they know about the problem. Encourage them to think about what type of solution would make sense for this type of problem. Remember, your role here is not to provide answers. It is to clarify the questions the employee is trying to answer, push them to consider new perspectives, and help them reflect on what they've learned.

16

Delegate as a Chance to Teach

For many managers, the hardest part of delegating is trusting that a task will be done well. But it becomes easier when you think of it as a chance to train your staff—not just get rid of some work. The next time you need to delegate something, start by determining who on your team is ready to handle more responsibility. Then create simple tasks to help them learn the skills they'll need. If you'd like someone to take over running a weekly meeting, for instance, have them practice each part of the process: one week, they can create an agenda, which you'll review. The next, they can watch you run the meeting, with plenty of chances to ask questions. Eventually they'll be ready to try running the meeting themselves, after which you can offer feedback. This kind of teaching can be time consuming, but it will go a long way toward preparing your team for more-complex work.

Make Team Learning Easier

Leaders want employees to continue to learn and develop new skills, but this wish will fail if you don't give people extra support. You might encourage employees to sign up for extra training and courses, but not many people will have time to engage properly, or at all, if their workloads remain the same and they have to study after hours. To promote more team learning, give them opportunities to develop. Give them stretch assignments and more autonomy. Make sure your team has access to resources to learn and grow, including people. Use mentoring to connect younger stars with seasoned executives; they can learn from each other. Establish regular check-ins for feedback, and measure progress through 360s. You can also fuel development by giving rewards such as promotions and stock ownership.

18

Shake Up an Employee's Routine

Every job contains some grunt work. If you manage someone who thinks they have more than their fair share, consider ways to change their responsibilities. You might, for example, impose a time constraint on an unglamorous task: Tell them the previous week's data needs to be compiled and reported by Monday at 4 p.m. Expect some pushback, since the employee is likely to say they can't complete the work in half the time. But ask them to at least try; a time constraint can turn an unexciting task into an engaging challenge. You should also consider assigning them some new work. Giving them more-exciting projects will compel them to get through their lower-value work more quickly. And share the burden: if employees see you doing grunt work, they'll be less likely to complain about it.

19

Recognize Your Employees' Achievements

Leaders have to actively build a sense of connectedness with their employees, and this starts with expressing appreciation.

- *Notice employees' unique contributions.* Say something that highlights something specific: "I appreciate the way you pull in people from other departments to reach your team goals. You're a connector."
- *Thank people personally and publicly.* Daily interactions—from the elevator to the parking lot—are opportunities to show appreciation for your employees' efforts. Public recognition at a staff meeting or a thoughtful "thank you" in a newsletter or email are also meaningful.

- *Ask "What do you think?"* Give people the opportunity to express themselves and be recognized for their ideas. Proactively ask employees, "How do you think we could improve?" and "What is keeping us stuck?"

20

What Not to Say When an Employee Makes a Mistake

Past-focused questions, like "What were you thinking?" only reinforce the mistake and make the person feel defensive. Instead, ask a question that looks forward: "How will you do it differently next time?" Focusing on the future this way allows the person to acknowledge their mistake and demonstrate what they've learned. It shows that you're confident in the person's abilities and gives you the chance to point out any problems in their thinking. Future-focused questions aren't easy to ask when your emotions are hot. Take a deep breath before speaking and remember that your goal in this situation is to help the employee grow, not to make them feel worse than they already do.

21

Take Responsibility for Your Team's Burnout

No manager wants a stressed-out team. And while employees have some responsibility to monitor their stress levels, leaders need to play a critical role in preventing and remedying burnout. Start with curiosity. Ask yourself: What is making my staff so unhealthy? How can I help them flourish? Then, gather data by asking your team what causes them to feel motivated or frustrated. Employees may not have a silver-bullet solution, but they can most certainly tell you what isn't working, and that is often very helpful data. Then, ask your team what they need. Think about small changes, for example, asking: If we had this much budget and could spend it on X many items in our department, what would be the first priority? Have the team vote anonymously, and then share the data with everyone. Discuss what was prioritized and why, and then start working down the list, performing small pilots and assessing what works. The good news is that burnout is preventable, and these low-risk and inexpensive experiments will give you useful information about what you need to change in your work environment.

22

Help Employees Return Smoothly from Medical Leave

When an employee returns from a medical leave, it's your job to help them ease back into work. The process starts during the leave: check in with the employee a few times so that they don't feel cut off from the team. When they're ready to return, come up with a transition plan and think through the precise details. For example, ask the employee how they want their return announced and talk about any schedule changes needed. Make sure to phase the transition plan, since the person may not be ready to return to 100 percent capacity right away. And consider how you can create a welcoming experience for their first day back. Once they're back, check in more frequently than you normally would to make sure they feel supported.

23

Help Your Team Be Themselves at Work

Many employees downplay their differences from each other at work to avoid drawing unwanted attention or making others uncomfortable. If you help your team members feel comfortable being themselves, they can focus on work rather than on hiding parts of their identities.

- *Shift the language.* When organizations talk about diversity, people tune out. Introduce the concept of "covering," or hiding certain aspects of yourself, to not appear different. Most people have done it at some point in their careers. This opens up a new way to talk about differences.

- *Share your story.* Most of us have had experiences related to covering, whether we faced it ourselves or witnessed it in someone close to us. Start the dialogue and let others know it's OK to do the same.

- ***Force the conversation.*** Build genuine connections with your employees, and speak up if they believe the corporate culture encourages covering.

24

Decrease the Bias in Your Hiring Decisions

Human beings are hardwired to prefer people who are like us, which is one reason bias creeps into hiring decisions. Diversity initiatives and process audits can help, but for hiring to improve meaningfully, individual managers have to recognize and address their personal biases. The first step is to accept that you have biases. Think about why you might feel drawn to some job candidates more than others, and what biases or preferences might be involved. Consider how factors such as race, gender, education, socioeconomic background, and even height might influence you. Aim to go into hiring decisions with an awareness of how they might go astray. Then, when you're actually evaluating a candidate, keep asking yourself: "Where could bias show up in this decision?" You should also form your own opinion of the candidate before comparing notes with your colleagues, so you aren't influenced by others' views.

25

Ease the Transition to Managing Former Peers

Being promoted into a manager position is exciting, but it can be awkward if your new team is made up of your former peers. When you're promoted over people who have always been friends (or rivals), the power relationship is inevitably altered. Here's how to ease the transition:

- *Meet with each team member one-on-one.* Individual meetings let you personalize your message and be more candid than a group setting allows. Talk to each person about what they do and how you can help them.

- *Hold a team meeting.* Using some ideas from the one-on-ones, discuss the purpose of the team, what should change, and what should stay the same. Explain how you like to operate and how you want your team to work together.

- *Deal swiftly with challenges to your authority.* If someone resists your leadership or goes behind your back, state your displeasure firmly and ask what's causing their dissent.

Lighten Your Team's Load

Project overload is real. But as a leader, you can find it hard to tell whether your team needs more resources or just could be working more efficiently. Ask people to identify their key activities and how much time they spend on them in a typical week. Use that data to assess workloads and priorities. Consider which tasks the team could stop doing and which might benefit from rethinking their process. Pay special attention to low-value projects that have to get done but that take an inordinate amount of time. Are there ways to simplify the workflows to reduce the amount of time your team spends in these areas? And look for tasks that simply can be done more quickly. If your team is still struggling after these steps, it might be time to hire more people.

Be a Mediator, Not a Boss, to Resolve Employee Conflicts

Two of your team members have had a disagreement that has escalated from a squabble to a full-blown argument, and now they want you to resolve it. What's the best way for you to step in? Your instinct might be to immediately fix the problem by making an executive decision, but your team will benefit more if you intervene as a mediator. Ask your colleagues to engage in a mediation process with you. Explain your hope that everyone will work together to find a resolution. And set a ground rule that they should focus on reaching agreement, not on persuading you that one of them is right. Taking this mediator approach will enable your colleagues to resolve the conflict themselves, making them less dependent on you to sort out future problems, and making it more likely that they'll follow through on the solution. In most workplace arguments, dictating a solution is less effective in the long run than showing your employees how to talk through their concerns together.

28

Help a Direct Report Clarify Their Career Goals

As a manager, helping your direct reports achieve their career goals is part of your job. But what do you do if they aren't sure what those goals are? First, tell the person that it's OK—and sometimes even preferable—not to have a concrete career path in mind. Being overly attached to a specific plan can cause people to miss opportunities that aren't on the prescribed route. Next, ask questions to understand what drives the employee, such as, "What problems excite you?" and "What types of work do you want to do less of and more of?" From there, encourage them to think about the skills they'll need in the future, focusing on those that will be transferable to other jobs or roles. Then suggest they try small experiments to learn more about what they like to do and where they need to develop.

29

Offer a Change of Scenery to a Mid-Career Employee

The mid-career crisis is a real phenomenon. People's satisfaction bottoms out when they're in the middle of their careers. As a manager, you don't want to lose these valuable employees just because they fall into a slump. To keep them engaged, consider offering a change of scenery through remote work or even a relocation. Remote work can let them change their personal lives without hurting their professional progress. A relocation to a different office could make sense for both the company and the employee if that office needs the employee's skills. Of course, a relocation is a big life change, so the company should be ready to assist with the move. In offering these options, you can help an experienced employee who still has years left in their career rekindle their enthusiasm for work.

Support Your Team's Mental Health

Mental health issues affect one in four adults. But when a colleague or direct report confides in you about an issue, you might find it hard to know the right way to respond. You can help in a few ways. Offer training to employees in how to support their colleagues. Training can teach people to recognize the signs of anxiety, depression, and other common mental health issues. They can also provide a safe space for role-playing so that employees can practice different scenarios. You can also create and share a list of trusted, publicly available resources for information and 24/7 advice. People often worry about the stigma that accompanies mental health issues, so tools they can use anonymously are valuable. By taking these steps, you can offer another essential kind of support: signaling that mental health issues, and the employees who struggle with them, matter.

Get Your Team to Be More Experimental

The most innovative companies encourage their employees to experiment. If you'd like to push your team to be more entrepreneurial, start by encouraging people to bring their outside interests to work. Ask your employees about their hobbies. What do they enjoy doing on weekends? What are they proud of outside of work? Employees who feel comfortable expressing their full, authentic selves are often better at coming up with new ideas. Creating a culture of experimentation also requires a fairly hands-off approach to leadership. Don't be a micromanager. Instead, show employees that you trust them to get work done, even in ways that haven't been tried before. When people have a sense of ownership, they feel more freedom to try something new. And finally, get comfortable with failure. People won't take risks if they're afraid of what will happen if a project doesn't work out. Measure someone's performance by their level of ingenuity, not their ability to play it safe.

32

Ask Your Employees More Questions

As you move up in an organization, people increasingly look to you for answers. But the best leaders don't provide all of the solutions; they inspire curiosity, creativity, and deeper thinking in their employees. And that starts with asking the right questions. Encourage your employees to slow down and explain what they're proposing in more detail by saying something simple and to the point, like "Wait, what?" You could also use phrases like "I wonder why . . . " to encourage curiosity. And then follow up with "I wonder if things could be done differently." Another question to try: "How can I help?" This question forces your colleague to define the problem, which is the first step toward owning and solving it.

33

Give Feedback Based on Facts, Not Opinions

When you give feedback on a fellow employee, it should be useful. But unless you connect it to what matters to them—and separate it from your personal beliefs and preferences—they won't be able to act on it. Emphasize facts, not interpretations. Stay away from subjective comments: "She's self-centered." "He lacks confidence." Even if you believe an employee's behavior stems from lack of confidence, for example, that's just your opinion; it may be inaccurate. Point to specific behaviors instead: "He doesn't contribute during meetings." "She interrupts me when I'm speaking." And ensure your feedback is both negative and positive, which helps to counteract your personal biases and preferences. For a colleague to improve, they need to know what they are doing well and where they have room to grow.

34

Don't Give Feedback When You Don't Need To

Feedback should be a regular part of work, but not every behavior warrants input. For example, you shouldn't offer corrective feedback just because someone has a different work process, even if it stresses you out. Before you deliver feedback, think about what you want to achieve. Avoid giving it when:

- You do not have all the information.
- It's something the recipient can't control.
- The person appears to be highly emotional or especially vulnerable.
- You don't have time to explain it thoroughly.

- It's based on a personal preference, not a need for more effective behavior.
- You don't have a solution for how the person can move forward.

35

Encourage Your Employees to Share What They Know

Many of us hide what we know at work because we don't want to lose the power or status that we think the knowledge gives us. But recent research shows that hoarding information often backfires and can negatively impact the withholder's growth and development. Your job is to create a culture in which your employees feel comfortable sharing information and speaking openly about their concerns. One way to figure out why your staff is holding back information is to use third-party, anonymous surveys. Then act on this feedback to gain back their trust. And make sure the people you manage understand the consequences of hiding knowledge. Those who are keeping information in order to protect themselves may not understand that they are actually doing the opposite. Use trainings, newsletters, bulletin boards, and other communication channels to help employees understand why sharing knowledge with your teammates is important.

36

Set Boundaries to Manage the Endless Stream of Emails

One of the reasons email is so hard to manage is that sending it is easy. We can fill up each other's inboxes by just clicking a button, which is why it's important to set boundaries around email. Try these three things:

- *Use autoreplies.* When you need time to focus on work, your email autoreply can tell people that you're unavailable and when you'll get back to them. Whether you'll reply in a day or a week, let people know what to expect. (And in the meantime, give yourself permission to ignore messages that can wait.)

- *Set guidelines for your team.* Tell people how and when you prefer to communicate, and ask colleagues and clients about their preferences as well. Don't forget to revisit this discussion when people join the team or new projects begin.

- *Lead by example.* If you answer emails late at night or on weekends, you're telling your team to do the same. Use services that allow you to schedule emails to send later. Better yet, step away from your inbox entirely.

37

For Better Virtual Meetings, Focus on Relationships

As more employees work offsite, virtual meetings are a necessity. "Reading the room" can be hard when you're not in the same room as your team, making these meetings tricky to navigate. Focus on building relationships. Allow ten minutes at the start for people to connect and catch up. This is your virtual watercooler time when you can have informal conversations. Ask questions about personal lives and families to get to know each other outside of work. Once you officially start the meeting, refer to each contributor by name so that everyone feels recognized and part of the community. When you can, meet face-to-face with the team. These techniques are the foundation for authentic conversation and connection, leading to more-effective virtual meetings.

38

Let Your Team Speak Their Minds in Meetings

When people feel safe enough to speak their minds in meetings, everyone benefits: employees get to be honest, and managers get to hear what their team members really think. Leaders can invite candid conversation by doing two things. First, focus on permission. Give people permission to say or ask anything they want. Sometimes in meetings it's unclear who is allowed to say what, or which topics people can and can't ask about. Discuss these things with your team up front. Ask your team for permission to lead the meeting—whether that means calling on people who haven't spoken, keeping the conversation on track, or holding people back if they're talking too much. Second, create psychological safety.

Everyone has had the experience of not feeling heard or respected; show your team that won't happen in your meetings. Ask the group to devote their full attention to whoever is talking, to not interrupt each other, and to highlight the value in other people's contributions.

39

Think about the Weight Your Words Carry

You have a lot of influence on how employees spend their time. Consider the ripple effects your input can have. Think of your comments, suggestions, and questions as pebbles you're throwing into a stream: Each one can have an impact far larger than you may intend. Always recognize the weight your words carry and speak with intention. During meetings with your team, don't think out loud, and lob ideas at everyone. Be sure you're giving the team a clear, unified picture of projects and strategies; if you aren't ready to do that, hold off on saying anything until you are. And don't ask for updates unless you really need them. Always specify what information you need, why, and when, so you don't create an unnecessary fire drill.

40

Make Kindness a Norm on Your Team

We all want to work in a place where people treat each other with kindness and respect. But you can't expect your team to behave that way without making it clear that you want them to. This process starts when you interview potential team members: tell candidates that your team values civility, so they can opt in to working for an organization where those values are prized. Have discussions with team members about what civility means and define the norms that you expect everyone to uphold daily. Compile those norms into a "civility code," which your employees can use as a guide. Once the norms are established, reinforce them however you can—in team meetings, at important events, and through rewards. These conversations and efforts garner buy-in and empower employees to hold one another accountable for civil behavior.

41

Don't Solve Your Team's Problems for Them

If your team is constantly bringing issues to you rather than addressing them on their own, you aren't doing your job as a manager. Only let problems get escalated to you thoughtfully and occasionally. Make sure you're not stepping in when you shouldn't. Don't ask yourself, "How do we solve the problem?" until you've paused and considered, "Who should own this problem?" Balance the need to resolve the issue with consideration for how your actions will influence future behavior. In your desire to help your team, you might be tempted to do more than you should. If others are struggling to solve problems they should rightfully own, always ask, "What is the least I can do?" Find the lowest level of initiative for yourself, while requiring your team members to act in ways they are capable of.

42

Give Your Employees Time and Space to Focus

Between scanning our inboxes, checking our phones, and feeling overwhelmed by our workloads, it's a wonder anyone can get work done. To help your employees focus and stay productive, you need to counterbalance these distractions. First, make sure the office has designated spaces where employees can disconnect. You don't have to install nap pods like Google—you can set aside a corner with comfy chairs or rooms where people can close the door and work. Second, encourage employees to block out chunks of focus time on their calendars. Tell them it's OK to ignore email or Slack for a few hours; have them use an auto-reply to let people know they're unavailable. ("I'm stepping away from my email to finish this project.

I'll be back in one hour.") And set policies for how quickly employees have to respond to messages. The more time they're spending on urgent emails, the less time they're spending on deep work.

43

Balance Your Team's Work Styles

As a leader, it's important to understand your work style and the styles of your employees. Prioritizers focus on goals, deadlines, and facts. Planners ask how the project will be delivered and completed. Arrangers want to know who the stakeholders are and who else should be involved. Visualizers consider why the project matters and what the end of the project will look like. All four types of people bring a valuable perspective to the table, and companies need all four types to remain competitive. Realistically, your team probably won't have a balance of all four styles, but you can bring on new members or call in outside experts to bridge the gaps. And if your team is heavily weighted toward one or two styles, recognize the value in balancing it. Work-style diversity ensures you'll have people focusing on both the big picture and the details.

44

Help Your Team Make Better Decisions

Judgment is a muscle that you can help your team build. Talk through how you make important decisions. Explain the criteria and stakeholders you consider, as well as any risks and trade-offs you assess to teach people how you think, help them understand company priorities, and demonstrate the factors to consider when making future judgment calls. Acknowledge that mistakes will happen, and that it's OK. Let your team members occasionally make big or hard decisions on their own. Remind yourself of your mistakes that helped you grow. Be curious, not dismissive, when a team member makes a poor judgment call. Ask questions to understand their thought process and push their thinking for next time.

45

Your B-Level Players Deserve Your Attention, Too

Every manager would love to have a team of A players, but that's probably not realistic. You're almost always going to have a mix of performers on your team, so make sure you're not ignoring your B players. These employees can be selfless, dedicated employees who fill important roles, but often they don't get the attention they deserve. Make sure you're giving them enough support and guidance by learning about their concerns, preferences, and work styles. Occasionally reassess their job fit to make sure they're in roles that draw on their strengths. And don't overlook someone's talents just because the person is quiet or reserved, or because they don't fit your idea of what a leader should act like. Some B players aren't comfortable in the spotlight but thrive when they're encouraged to complete a project or to contribute for the good of the company. When they have the motivation and the encouragement they need, B players can turn in an A+ performance.

46

Lead Your B-Level Players to A-Level Success

Can a team of B players achieve A+ success? Research says yes, but only with an A-level leader. As an effective leader, you can have a variety of styles, with certain characteristics: superior judgment, which helps you make good decisions and learn from mistakes; high emotional intelligence, which helps you stay calm under pressure and build relationships with your teams; and high ambition, which pushes you to high performance. In addition, you can use four tactics to make your teams more effective: Have a strong vision that motivates your team with a plan of attack and milestones. Use analytics to help your team make smarter, better decisions with data. Give honest feedback about team members' limits and help them improve.

And foster morale by encouraging team bonding. When people care about each other, they raise their performance for each other, too.

47

Staff Your Big New Project with Three Kinds of People

When you're staffing a high-profile project, you want an all-star team. But it's not enough to put your high performers on the task. There are three types of people who should be on the team of any breakthrough initiative. First, look for employees who are comfortable with uncertainty. You need individuals who will remain curious and focused even when the project is far from the end goal. Second, be sure you have people who create structure within chaos and take action. These workers can drive a team forward even when circumstances change. Finally, find employees who have a combination of these critical traits: divergent thinking (the ability to connect seemingly unrelated information and ideas); convergent action (the ability to execute on ideas and create something tangible); and influential communication (the ability to share knowledge in a coherent, compelling way). Many people have one of these critical traits, but your project team needs employees who have all of them.

48

Protect Your High Performers from Burnout

When a high performer on your team burns out, you might think it's their problem to solve. But your job is to help employees control their stress. You can protect your stars by giving them some autonomy in choosing their projects. Don't just put them on the toughest tasks; letting them choose ensures they're working on assignments that excite them. Pair the person with another high performer on a hard project, which will help them challenge and push each other. The pairs should be employees at similar levels.

49

Give Opportunities to Your Top Employees

Every manager wants to keep their stars. One of the best ways to win loyalty from your top talent is to give them as many opportunities as you can. Let them take on big challenges like a highly visible project or a new leadership role. You may have to battle HR to make this happen. After all, HR leaders tend to want to treat people homogeneously and limit opportunities to rigid time frames. They may insist that your star isn't ready, or that giving the role to the star isn't fair to others who are more senior. You can promise to look for opportunities for those you've bypassed and take full responsibility for what your top talent is—and isn't—able to do. Don't let red tape stand in your way. If your top talent is blocked and made to wait for opportunity to be available, they will simply go somewhere else.

50

What to Do Before Telling Someone They're Fired

Telling someone they're fired is never easy, but you can take steps to make it less painful. Before starting the conversation, make sure you've prepared responsibly. Does the person know there's been an issue? Have they been given an opportunity to act on your feedback? Identify the right environment for the meeting—a private place where you won't be interrupted. Think about what you want to say. Instead of preparing a script, focus on setting your intentions. Really think about the person: who they are, why you hired them, what this will be like for them. Try to see the best in the other person. Imagine them contributing more powerfully in another organization or role. And approach the conversation with the assumption that they have value—it may just be in a different job.

51

Don't Be Afraid to Show Some Emotion

Keeping a cool head at work is important for decision making and team cohesion, but it can have an unintended drawback: your calm professional persona may be so rigid that you forget to be yourself or show your emotions. As a leader, it's hard to generate enthusiasm among your direct reports if you always wear a serious face. Next time you prepare for an important speech or meeting, think about the emotional takeaway you want to impart to your employees. Then choose words that match your emotional tone. If you want your team to feel confident, for example, say you are "proud" and their ideas are "powerful." Or if your team is facing a tight deadline, tell them the task is "critical" and you're "eager" to meet the opportunity so that your organization won't "miss out." Without emotional language, your message may fall flat, so be forthcoming about how you feel; a leader's emotions are contagious. If you project excitement or encouragement, your team will pick up on your energy.

Challenge Your Employees to Keep Them Engaged

Leaders play a significant role in helping employees understand why their jobs matter, but it's not just about connecting their work to a larger purpose. You can also do it by demonstrating curiosity: explore, ask questions, and engage people on their ideas about the future. Make clear that there is a wide range of possibilities for how work gets done and that you want your employees to try new things. At the same time, keep them focused on meeting goals and making progress. Remain ambitious in the face of both failure and success, and push your people to continually accomplish more. You want employees to feel a sense of progress, reinvention, and growth, which results in a more meaningful and positive work experience.

53

Build Your Team's Trust

To be effective, leaders need their team's trust. But how do you get that trust—and how do you get it back if you've lost it? Three behaviors are essential. First, create positive relationships on your team. Help employees cooperate, resolve conflicts between others, give honest feedback, and check in with people about their concerns. Second, demonstrate expertise and judgment. People are more likely to trust you if they believe you have technical know-how and the experience to make good decisions about the team's work. Last, be consistent. You must do what you say you will do. Follow through on your commitments and keep any promises you make. You don't need to be perfect at these three behaviors to be a trusted leader, but you do need to be good at them.

Explain How You Make Decisions

Most managers dedicate significant amounts of time and energy to ensuring they're being fair. But it's inevitable that some will perceive outcomes as fair, and others, as unfair. Be transparent about how and why you made a decision. For example, if you want an equitable promotions process, with certain competencies or styles counting more than others, tell your team your intentions. If you want equal sharing of bonuses, to reinforce the importance of every employee, be up front about it. As the manager, you have the discretion to make those decisions. As long as you have thought carefully about what the business needs, and made your decision as objectively as possible, you have done your job. You'll always have an opportunity to restore balance with the next decision.

55

Help Your Team Avoid Unhealthy Competition

Collaborating is hard if you view your colleague as the competition. Even when leaders don't explicitly paint a win-lose game for their teams, the competitive mindset is the default for most high-achieving professionals. So you have to communicate the message that success in the team can be greater and more exciting when people work together. Emphasize the opportunity for all team members to value and learn from each other. And follow these tactics to help employees adopt a teaming mindset:

- Model the behavior you're hoping to inspire. Demonstrate curiosity and interest in the people you work with, ask them genuine questions, and respond thoughtfully to what you hear.

- Place a high value on and reward successful teaming more than individual performance.
- Frame the challenge ahead (the work, the initiative, the project) as something in need of diverse perspectives and skills.

56

Don't Let Envy Be Part of Your Team's Culture

Nothing good comes of envy. If employees are resentful about what they feel they deserve or what others have, morale and well-being will suffer. You can combat envy by building a culture of goodwill ("I'm grateful for what I have, and happy about your success") rather than one of comparison ("I deserve what you have"). Start by setting an example. Let your team see you supporting your peers and cheering their accomplishments. Show employees that you value genuine camaraderie, and encourage them to measure themselves by their own achievements rather than by others'. Discuss how people can combat feelings of envy (and even how you've managed envy in the past). For example, employees may benefit from talking with a friend or mentor to dissect what they're feeling and regain perspective. They should also try to avoid unhealthy comparisons and the distorted perspectives that come with them. A culture in which people want each other to succeed is one that can bring out the best in everyone.

57

Don't Let a Toxic Culture Drag Down Your Team

Company culture exerts a powerful influence on employees' behavior. In some cases, that power can turn toxic, driving us to compromise our values and do things we normally wouldn't. You probably can't change a toxic culture on your own, but there are steps you can take to insulate yourself from its effects. First, figure out the kind of environment you need to be effective—and happy—at work. Which of your values have fallen by the wayside? Do you feel healthy and content? Are you proud of how you behave toward colleagues? Next, talk to your teammates about the culture you all wish you had. Ask what's important to them at work and how company norms have affected their behavior. Then talk about establishing and committing to a team "microculture" based on everyone's shared values. The microculture may not fix the company's broader issues, but it can encourage your team members to resist the negative pressures they face in their jobs.

58

When to Change Your Employee's Goals

As a manager, what do you do if, after working hard with your employee to set goals at the beginning of the year, it's no longer clear that those targets are still worth pursuing? Perhaps your employee has achieved a goal and needs a new challenge, or the organization's objectives have changed. Meet with the employee to review the existing goals and plans. These questions can help guide your discussion and reassess the targets:

- Are the goals still realistic, given any changes in resources or constraints?
- Are they still timely? Is now the best time to achieve them?
- Are they still relevant? Do they still align with the company's strategy?

Depending on the answers, you may need to change only a single goal, replacing it with a new one—but in some cases, the entire plan might need to shift. Work collaboratively with your direct report to come up with new goals that are achievable and important to the organization.

59

During Change, Ask Employees What Worries Them

If you want to lead a successful organizational change, you have to communicate about the change empathetically. And that means finding out how your team feels and tailoring your emails and meetings to their concerns. Leaders who don't take this step risk alienating their employees, who may already be feeling nervous or skeptical. So talk to your team members about what's happening and why. Ask what they're worried about and what kind of improvements they'd like to see. Listen closely and then use your communications to address what you heard. Repeat these steps during each phase of the change, so you can gauge how people's feelings are shifting over time. The goal is to make sure everyone feels included and heard. You should also be as transparent about the change as possible. It's likely that you'll need to keep some details about the how and why private, but being open will build trust and credibility.

60

Ask Your Team the Right Questions

Being a strategic leader starts with asking your team the right questions about their work, your company, and the big picture. Here are five questions to pose to team members on a regular basis:

- *What are you doing today?* This will bring to light any significant work that you aren't aware is being done or that's taking much more time than it should.
- *Why are you doing the work you're doing?* This allows you to gain clarity on what's important and why it's important from your team's perspective.
- *How does what we're doing today align with the bigger picture?* This is a discussion about gaps and outliers. If your team is working on something that doesn't align with the broader goals of the organization, challenge the value of doing that work.

- *What does success look like for our team?* This allows you to home in on what's really driving your team's success, in terms of activities, behaviors, relationships, and strategic outcomes.
- *What else could we do to achieve more, better, faster?* This is where you push your team to be innovative. If you've done the work to answer the preceding questions, you are well positioned to be strategic in answering this one.

Attributions

Managing Yourself

1. "How to Stop Worrying about What Other People Think of You," by Michael Gervais
2. "How to Lead When You're Feeling Afraid," by Peter Bregman
3. "3 Simple Habits to Improve Your Critical Thinking," by Helen Lee Bouygues
4. "To Achieve Big Goals, Start with Small Habits," by Sabina Nawaz
5. "How to Manage Your Perfectionism," by Rebecca Knight
6. "You're Never Going to Be 'Caught Up' at Work. Stop Feeling Guilty about It," by Art Markman
7. "The Case for Finally Cleaning Your Desk," by Libby Sander
8. "Learning Is Supposed to Feel Uncomfortable," by Peter Bregman
9. "Making Learning a Part of Everyday Work," by Josh Bersin and Marc Zao Sanders
10. "How to Stop Obsessing over Your Mistakes," by Alice Boyes

Managing Your Team

21. "Burnout Is about Your Workplace, Not Your People," by Jennifer Moss
22. "How to Welcome an Employee Back from Medical Leave," by Anne Sugar
23. "Help Your Employees Be Themselves at Work," by Christie Smith and Dorie Clark
24. "How to Reduce Personal Bias When Hiring," by Ruchika Tulshyan
25. "What to Do First When Managing Former Peers," by Liane Davey
26. "What to Do If Your Team Is Too Busy to Take On New Work," by Dutta Satadip
27. "How to Handle a Disagreement on Your Team," by Jeanne Brett and Stephen B. Goldberg
28. "How to Mentor Someone Who Doesn't Know What Their Career Goals Should Be," by Tania Luna and Jordan Cohen
29. "Many Employees Have a Mid-Career Crisis. Here's How Employers Can Help," by Serenity Gibbons
30. "What Companies Can Do to Help Employees Address Mental Health Issues," by Barbara Harvey
31. "How to Encourage Entrepreneurial Thinking on Your Team," by Sergei Revzin and Vadim Revzin
32. "5 Questions Leaders Should Be Asking All the Time," by James E. Ryan
33. "How to Give Feedback People Can Actually Use," by Jennifer Porter
34. *Giving Effective Feedback* (HBR 20-Minute Manager Series)

Index